# SPRING LAUGHTER

Also by the Author:

*Timeless Moment*
*Upland Pastures*

# CHRISTINA RAINSFORD

# *Spring Laughter*

THE GOLDEN QUILL PRESS
*Publishers*

Francestown          New Hampshire

Library of Congress Catalog Card Number 80-66877

ISBN 0-8233-0316-0

Printed in the United States of America

## ACKNOWLEDGMENTS

Some of these poems have appeared in the following publications and thanks are due them for permission to reprint: *The New York Times, The Christian Science Monitor, The Classical Outlook, The Columbus Citizen, The Denver Post, The Educational Forum, Fiesta Magazine, Imprints Quarterly* and *Lyric.*

# CONTENTS

## *Songs of the Seasons*

## *Places and People*

*Spring Laughter*

*Light Verse*

# SONGS OF THE SEASONS

# A COUNTRY-MAN'S CLOCK

He needs no calendar to mark the turn
of seasons.  Punctual as clocks the flowers appear
in their progression in the woods and fields
to tell the country-man the time of year:

Though ice still rims the edges of the pond,
the wind blows cold and branches are swept clean;
he knows that winter's past when in the swamp
skunk cabbages unfurl their brave spring green.

When birds return and boughs put on their leaves
and every apple tree is a bride's bouquet,
when in the woods the frail spring-beauties hide
among the fern, he knows that it is May.

Daisies whiten all the fields of June,
color's ablaze in meadows of July
where blackeyed-Susans flaunt their vivid gold
and chickory is like a fallen bit of sky.

Now August sees the milk-weed burst its pods,
along the roads the golden-rod grows tall
and soon late asters and the first red leaf
proclaim September and approaching fall.

## SUMMER IDYLL

Let us lie in the meadow
deep in the feathered grass.
Sun sifts down to warm the earth,
through tunnels of blades
a rabbit scurries,
a lady-bug climbs a tall stem
as I have seen a bronze boy
climb a palm-tree trunk.
A bobolink rises from his nest close by
to pour his song
on the clover-scented air.
We feel the pulse of growth,
the secret stratagem
of root and seed
as we lie in the tall grass
under a summer sky.

# WEEDS

Sing praise of weeds,
spendthrift flowers
that brighten roadsides
luring the butterflies,
tough grasses, anchoring shifting sands.
These need no gardener's care
but flourish in stubborn soil.
Dandelions raise bright heads
between cracks in concrete,
fire-weed turns charred ground
to purple splendor,
milk-weed leaves, soft as rabbit ears,
rise up between the rail-road ties,
woodbine throws green tendrils
over a rubbish heap,
prodigal, unconquerable weeds!

## SUMMER BALLET

Six dragonflies, green, gold and blue
dart and hover in the sun
above the glassy lake, each one
reflected there, a ballet corps
on gauzy wings, they sweep and soar,
poise on a water-lily pad
then rise and circle high
against the back-drop of the sky.

## LUNA MOTH

Green as jade,
soft as fur,
with jeweled eyes
and antlered head
the great moth came
out of the dark
to lie outspread
against the screen,
embodying
in its silent flight
all the mystery
of the night.

17

## MID-SUMMER

This is the lavish season,
spring's promises fulfilled,
all the secret growing
brought to flower and spilled,
prodigal, full-blown
upon the waiting earth.
Creatures of field and forest
have brought their young to birth,
spiders spread their cobwebs
dew-spangled on the lawn,
the buzz of unseen insects
vibrate from dusk to dawn
and in the darkening wood
fire-fly lanterns glimmer.
This is the lavish season
the high-tide of summer.

## WINGS

Before birds flew in the primordial sky
insects buzzed and hummed,
surviving through aeons of unrecorded time
to fill the summer air with wings
of infinite variety — the painted wings
of butterflies, poised on a flower,
opening and closing like a fan,
those of dragonflies, stiff and translucent,
darting over a pond,
quivering on a lily pad,
metallic wings of grasshoppers
in their whirring flight,
the small frail wings of bees,
dotted with pollen from a flower's heart.
The hum of insects vibrates through the day
but with night, moths come silently
in velvet flight.

# A SONG OF SUMMER'S END

These are the signs of summer's end,
birds gather for their southern flight
and the insistent katydid
shrills without pause throughout the night.

From his sojourn in the north
we welcome back the chickadees
apples rotting on the grass
lure the buzzing wasps and bees.

The milk-weed bursts its ripened pods
and sends its airy freight abroad,
alder berries are turning red,
asters bloom along the road.

Summer's passing, summer's passing
all these portents seem to say,
summer's passing, summer's passing,
make the most of every day.

## CONVOCATION OF CROWS

Raucous cawing filled the air,
obsidian wings beat overhead
crows so many and so near
filled me with atavistic dread.

Were these birds of evil portent?
Cawing, flapping they seemed to be
heralds of foreboding sent
to warn of some calamity.

But when they perched upon the trees
with sunshine on each glossy wing
my fears were gone.  I knew that these
were just the birds I'd known since spring,

and had no evil connotation
as they gathered there together
for their yearly convocation
in the bright October weather.

# INDIAN SUMMER

Through the windless air,
quiet as falling dew,
the last yellow leaves come drifting down.
They turn the woodland pathway
to a thread of gold
and launch bright argosies
to float down the swift-running stream.
On such a day,
like the hush that falls upon an audience
when the theater darkens,
all nature seems waiting in expectation
for winter's lusty drama
to begin.

# WINTER POND

No wind will walk upon the water now,
nor ripples flash like shoals of silver fish.
The pond is winter-locked from shore to shore.
But see — where the stream
cascades into its depths
the ice breaks into intricate designs,
and over-hanging branches washed with spray
turn into crystal filigree.
Those that think winter dull and harsh
should see his airy touch along the pond
as delicate as flowers.

# CHRISTMAS GREENS

In ancient days the Greeks and Romans
gathering on a festal day
to celebrate some pagan rite
brought leaves of laurel and of bay.

And now at Christmas time, we too
go to the woods across the snow
and bring back greens to deck the house
with laurel and with balsam bough.

In every century and clime
the evergreen has been held dear,
a symbol of enduring life
in the dark turning of the year.

# SNOW BLOOM

On a bitter day of lowering clouds
and leafless woods, my unbelieving eyes
saw a tree in flower.

Snow had filled the empty cups
of fallen hazel nuts with frosty petals
white as cherry bloom.

For their brief hour of blossoming
they touched the gloomy wood with spring,
May on a winter tree.

# GROSBEAKS

"Come to the window," she cried.
"Quickly, look outside,"
and there on the lawn I saw
grosbeaks by the score.
From somber skies they fell,
a winter miracle,
turning snow and ice
to tropic paradise.
The barren tree was loud
with chatter, its branches bowed
with the bright blossoming
of gauzy wing on wing.

# STAY-AT-HOME

Now is the season post cards come
from traveling friends
who fled the cold.
I look out at my snowy world
and do not envy them.
What sparkling tropic sea
can rival the brightness
of this field of snow?
What palm trees can compare
with these tall pines
bowed with their crystal bloom?
What statues mute in galleries
vie with these strange ice sculptures
glittering in frosty air?

There is time to watch our domestic sun
set each day further north
till it reaches the tulip tree
and starts its slow journey back
with lengthening days.
Time to savor joys of home
as drifts pile high,
the blazing fire, the waiting book,
the pot of tea brewing its drowsy spell.

I hear a plane drone overhead
bound for a distant land —
and wish it well.

# ICE STORM

The wind howled challenge to the trees,
we heard them battling through the night,
brittle clash of storm-tossed branches
broken in the fight.

We trembled as the wind blew fiercer
and knew by a sudden thunderous sound
that some great warrior of the years
was felled to ground.

When morning came the field lay silent,
foe routed and the battle won,
proud in victorious splendor
the trees shone in the sun.

# THE OPEN DOOR

March has opened the door to spring,
only a crack, but enough to let through
a crocus and a robin or two,
and melt the ice imprisoning
the brook. We hear its voice again.
Pines shake off their weight of snow,
buds swell on the naked bough,
an early wasp crawls on the pane.

Dearer than summer's rich bouquet
is the first flush on the maple tree,
sweeter than summer's symphony
the peepers on a warm March day.

# SPRING PEEPERS

The woodland symphony is tuning up,
from the marsh come the first tentative notes,
and suddenly the air is all alive
with joyous bubbling fron unseen throats.

Oh small musicians coming with the spring
out of the darkness since the world began,
your happy choruses have stirred men's hearts
hearing again the distant pipes of Pan,

when a new morning lay upon a world
innocent of terror and of pain.
All our forgotten springs are in your voice
and listening our hearts grow young again.

## EARLY WASP

Along the window ledge, a wasp
still winter-numb, crawls languidly,
not as in summer, when buzzing angrily
he flies about my head, competing
for the juicy peach I am eating.
I view him now with different eyes,
greeting him with pleased surprise
as a first sign of spring,
observing
his gauzy wings outstretched,
his golden body, etched
with black, tiered like a Chinese tower,
his sting with its latent power.
Now he crawls along the sun-warmed board,
harmless as a sheathed sword.

# PLACES AND PEOPLE

# A COUNTRY'S COLOR LINGERS IN THE MIND

Scotland speaks in muted tones,
sepia mist shrouding heathered hills,
brown shades of tweed
woven in crofters' cottages,
grey gulls over grey seas.

India's color is a trumpet call,
a crash of cymbals,
vivid green of rice paddies,
wreaths of marigolds
decking the heads
of women in gay saris,
sun glinting on brass water jars
and over all the intense blue sky.

Greece is a symphony of light,
no color lingers in the mind
only the classic light,
crystal in its purity.

# ABUNDANT WATER

I have come from an arid land
where the only water
is drawn from the village well
and carried home in brass pitchers
on the heads of women.
Now I am home I turn the tap on full
to watch the water rush in.
I dip my fingers in the spring
and feel the drops run through them
silvery and cool,
listen to the sound of the brook
and the lap of waves
on the shore of the lake.
I run out into the storm,
smell the damp earth
and feel the abundant water
on my uplifted face,
thinking of those women
and their water jars.

## PAVILION OF SHAH JEHAN, DELHI

Inlays of jade and of chalcedony,
lattice windows framing
the quiet flowing river,
and this inscription
carved upon the wall —
"If there is a heaven on earth
it is here, it is here."
Surely it was something other
than the beauty of the place
that caused the Shah to write these words,
some essence of content, some revelation
came to him here.

Blessed is the man who knows
such moments in his dwelling
and with true insight
looks at the home of his creation
and finds his heaven in its walls.

# GRECIAN ISLAND

Out of Homer's wine dark sea,
an island rose, our first sight
of Greece.  Two temple columns stood
bathed in classic light
upon a tawny cliff,
there was a curve of bay,
a gnarled olive tree,
all our dreams of Greece
in epitome.

From the little harbor, a boat
with orange sail was drifting west.
I thought of Ulysses' voyaging,
of Jason's quest.

Though tides of time have washed away
much from the life I left behind,
the first sight of that fabled land
is stamped forever on my mind.

# ITALIAN HILL TOWNS

These are the towns the Umbrian artists loved
as background scenes for the Nativity.
Time has not touched them through the centuries.
Women fill their pitchers at the fountain,
old men sit and doze and tap their pipes,
a patient frieze of age and timelessness.
Flowers cascade from walls and balconies
of houses the creamy color of old lace.
Pigeons wheel around the old clock-tower,
and up and down the narrow cobbled street
the mincing feet of donkeys tap a tune.
Beyond the town, vineyards terrace the hill
and great-flanked oxen take their ponderous way
with loaded wain just as in Virgil's day.

# TINTAGEL

Clouds hang low over Tintagel,
evoking its somber story
of passion and doomed love.
Castle walls and battlements
rise in their ruins
above the contending surf,
where gulls with melancholy cry
are keening an ancient grief.
The long line of the Cornish coast
dissolves in distance.  A ship looms
through the death-white fog
that hangs over the sea.
So through the mists of time
merging history and myth
glides with sails outspread
a phantom ship
bearing Iseult of Ireland
to the waiting king.

## AN IRISH WALK

We walked in the mist down an Irish lane.
Hedges of fuschia lined the way,
turning the ground to purple and red
where fallen blossoms lay.

We heard the sound of the distant sea,
baaing sheep among the heather;
pungent peat smoke drifted low
in the misty weather.

Passing a white thatched cottage
we caught a whiff of new-baked bread.
A woman stood in the open door,
" 'Tis a fine saft day," she said.

# JAMAICAN BEACH

Far out upon the reefs the breakers pound,
tossing their white spume in the sun,
guarding the tranquil bay whose waters lie
in shifting shades of turquoise and of blue.
In its clear depths small silver fishes dart,
safe from the threatening jaws
of open sea.

This is the lotus land where time is not.
The turmoil of the world breaks on the reefs
and is forgotten here.  Peace is a presence
and care transmuted by the alchemy
of sea and sky.

# THE ISLAND

On an island far at sea,
washed by waves continually,
I lay in the sun on a grassy cliff
smelt the salt and a tangy whiff
of bay and sweet-fern.  Sea birds flew
in wheeling arcs in the double blue
of sky and sea, while far below
the tides in rhythmic ebb and flow
sucked at pebbles on the beach.
Lapped by silence, out of reach
of city crowds and stridency
peace companioned me.

# THE SECRET PLACE

We never knew who owned this place
but our hearts claimed it —
this small secret glade
hidden by surrounding woods.
A crumbling wall told
where once a house had stood,
a lilac and gnarled apple tree
still blossomed sparely every spring.
It was a haunt for birds,
and deer came
to eat the small hard apples in the fall,
squirrels chattered from pine tree boughs
and seeds of nibbled cones
made a small patter as they fell.
We thought it would be ours always,
a hidden refuge,
but when we came again in spring
a distant whine warned what we would find.
Every tree was being felled,
all creatures of the wood were gone,
no growing thing found foothold
in the hard-packed level ground.
But from the severed apple tree,
undaunted, bloom had sprung.

# LONG ISLAND REVISITED

Names give false promise of delight,
"Ocean Vista", Bayberry Ridge",
here where identical houses
swelter in sun,
mangy grass struggles for a foothold
in arid soil,
picture windows frame the neighbor's wash,
a forest of antennae sprout from roofs.
Once, long ago,
we lay on the bluff and watched
the curve of sea-gull wings.
Do you remember the wide sky,
the stillness,
all of summer distilled
in scent of wild roses?
Do you remember?

# AT THE ZOO

## *I - The Buffalo*

"The only animal that stands
facing the storm", the keeper said.

I saw in my mind endless prairies
swept by blizzards from the north
and the great beasts standing
taking the blast,
snow whitening their manes.

I heard the bulls fighting,
pawing the ground and bellowing,
felt the earth shake
to the stamp of a thousand hooves
as they galloped free,
a dark river pouring over virgin land.

# AT THE ZOO

## *II - The Gazelle*

The gazelle had a broken horn,
only one adorned its head,
"Doubtless the way," the keeper said,
"the myth of the unicorn spread."

Quickly I turned away
and barred the gates of my mind
to keep the factual out
of that legendary land
where the milk-white unicorn
roamed the forest aisle
tapestried in flowers,
seeking a maiden without guile
and having found her, bowed
its head upon her knees
as she sat in virgin innocence
embowered by the trees
from whose laden branches
golden apples hung,
while sweetly on the air
rose the bird's primal song.

# STUDIES IN WHITE

I saw white clouds reflected
in the water of a pond
where two swans floated.
On the bank beyond
a fleet of small white butterflies
hovered with gossamer grace
over a clump of creamy
Queen Anne's lace.

Now swans are gone from the frozen pond,
banks piled high with drifted snow,
only some ice-encrusted stalks
tell where summer flowers grew.
Flakes fall swirling through the air
like silver butterflies in flight,
all else is blotted out
in a world of white.

## METAMORPHOSIS

The old house that stood so long
dark and untenanted
with broken windows, sagging shutters,
is alive again, healed of its wounds
by the new young owners and their love.
We watch them
busy with ladder, paint and hammer,
sunlight on shining windows,
a plume of smoke from the chimney.

On the lilac, buds are swelling.
Soon spring will come
and with green banners
and joyful song, celebrate
the turning of a house
into a home.

# OLD STONE WALLS

"Something there is
that does not love a wall",
said Robert Frost.
But who would not love
these weathered stones.
They mark no boundaries now,
keep nothing in or out
but stand, etched with lichen,
warm in summer sun,
festooned with scarlet woodbine
in the fall.
Built by the skill and toil
of men who farmed the land
a century ago,
the walls remain,
impervious to time,
symbol of permanence
in a changing world.

## THE CHANGING HILLS

The mountains stand, rooted in eternity,
yet change from hour to hour.
While the valley lies in darkness
the summits leap into light
taking the sun's first rays.
In the clarity of noon they stand,
bastions to the sky,
the ravines, wells of blackness
in the sun-lit slopes,
where cloud shadows pass
in slow procession.
At evening the great hills grow tender
suffused with a pink glow
and with the night
their summits touch the stars.

## CONSTRUCTION WORKER

His golden hair falls to his shoulders
under his hard hat, shaped like a helmet.
Put a shield on his breast
and he could be a Greek warrior.
He throws a blazing brand
instead of a javelin
and flirts with death
high above the city streets
instead of on the plains of Marathon.

## HOLD UP

His pockets held just fifty cents.
They fled with curses of disgust
and left him lying in the dust
for startled passersby to find.

Sprawled along the path he lay
in death's outrageous disarray.
A twisted smile was on his lips
as though he found it rather funny
to have been murdered for his money.

# FEAST OF THE PASSOVER

"Sell the candlesticks", they said,
when bills piled up and cash was low.
The mother cringed and shook her head.
She would never let them go.

The very thought was a sacrilege,
more than silver made their worth,
they were a symbol and a pledge
of adherence to her faith.

They laughed at her old-fashioned ways,
her children's ways bewildered her.
She sat alone through empty days
her faith both strength and comforter.

None came home to share the feast,
she lit the candles with a heart like stone
and laid the table with her best
and ate the bitter herbs alone.

# IN AN ALIEN LAND

I weep for those who through the centuries
fought and died in an alien land
dreaming of home. Hannibal's troops
far from palms and desert sand,
shivering with unaccustomed cold
as they prodded elephant and pack-ass
through the implacable snow
of an Alpine pass.

Caesar's legions longing for Rome
treated with scorn and enmity
by sullen tribes from Palestine
to Briton's northern sea.

Spaniards in Mexico, sun hot
on their helmets, sweating in cumbersome
armor through malarial swamps,
dreaming of home in their delirium.

Not only in the past but at this hour
men fight and fall
on foreign soil.
Weep for them all!

# THE OLD

Prodigal of the present,
the young lean to the future
having a meager store of memories.
Not so the old, who know how swiftly
spring turns to summer, summer to fall,
fall to winter and a year is gone.
Each beauty of the earth,
each fleeting joy, is doubly dear,
the flight of homing birds
against the sunset sky,
a child's spontaneous hug.
Friendship and love have a new poignancy
and the beloved dead seem closer now
as the gap between them narrows.
As a pond, no longer ruffled by wind
mirrors the sky, their minds,
stilled of the tumults of youth
reflect the past,
sorrows softened by time,
joys enhancing the present.

## FIRST SNOW

Lately come from Africa,
young Abdul stops amazed
at white feathers falling from the sky.
He reaches up to catch them as they pass,
astonished when they disappear
within his grasp,
leaving his fingers cold.
He knows the silence of the desert,
but this is deeper stillness,
all sounds muffled in whirling white.
He stands with face uplifted
his black eyes big with wonder.

# GROCERY BOY

On a dreary day I heard him pass
pushing a grocery cart,
singing a gay Italian air
from a merry heart.

The people hurrying on their way
smiled as they heard him sing,
the sky seemed suddenly less grey
and dismal thoughts took wing.

I marveled at the power of song
to weave a potent spell,
if a passing grocery boy
could work this miracle.

## SKIERS

Lovely as the flight of birds,
the sweep of skiers as they go
flying down the mountain side,
black against dazzling snow.

I watch them from the road beneath
and all my being envies them,
high in that snowy solitude
above the world of men.

# WHAT?

"It will never work",
I heard him say to the woman
as I left the bus.
All day the question
buzzed in my mind
like a fly above a honey pot.
What wouldn't work?
Were they contemplating marriage?
I conjured up fatal objections
to such a step.
Was it a business venture
with dazzling possibilities
but fraught with pit-falls,
or a daring plan for a robbery,
or, more prosaically
did he prick the bubble
of her enthusiasm for a new gadget
with the disheartening word,
"It will never work"?
I will never know.

## SALES GIRL

She stood behind the counter
piled high with games and toys,
on her lips was scarlet
and in her eyes were boys.

With romance always beckoning
in this exciting city,
to be behind a counter
really seemed a pity.

She waited on me listlessly
and I could sympathize —
how could she take an interest
in my mundane supplies,

when the boy she met last evening
waited for her 'round the block?
Her heart was there already,
it was nearly five o'clock.

# PERIOD PIECE – THE DANCING CLASS

As it is snowing, mother orders a cab.
Penelope, patent-leather shoes
in an embroidered bag,
snuggles into the heavy rug,
smelling of stable.
The dressing room is a flutter of sashes,
butterfly bows and bobbing curls.

The pianist plays a polka, waltzes –
one, two, three, turn,
one, two, three, turn.
The dancing master, svelte and elegant
in swallow-tails, bows to Penelope
as she curtsies.

In the grand march, Penelope and her partner
in Eton suit and wide collar
move sedately past gilt mirrors
and chattering mothers in hats
heavy with ostrich plumes.

# FRAGMENTS

The waves of time have washed away
much of childhood memories,
but some remain.
Vivid as yesterday
I still can see the pattern
moonlight made upon my nursery bed,
the burst of flame, a golden flower,
when mother lit the gas-jet
in my room.
Feel the shiver, half fear
half delight
as the small cold hand
of the organ grinder's monkey
took my proffered coin.
Hear the clanging bell
and galloping hooves
of fire engines thundering
down the street.
Smell the Christmas scent
of balsam and burning wax
as I stood in awe
beside our candle-lighted tree.

## LETTER TO YOUNG LOVERS

Young men, bearded and debonair,
beautiful girls with fountains of hair,
unabashed in your embraces,
undeterred by public places,
scorning all formality,
a different breed you seem to be
from that of my far youthful days.
But, though expressed in other ways,
love is the same the ages through.
We walked on air the same as you,
holding hands gave us the bliss
you find in your more passionate kiss,
and when the tender moment came
to be addressed by our first name
instead of the more formal "Miss",
we thought our hearts would overflow.
Dear young lovers as you go
arm in arm along the street
walking as on winged feet,
happy lovers if you but knew
all my heart goes there with you.

## SHOPPER

The orbit of her days was small,
local concerns, gossip with friends
over a drug-store coke.
She fitted to its size and found it good.
Her marriage to a New Yorker
made headlines in the local paper.
Now, lost in this planetary city,
she misses the familiar round.
Alone, after the morning goodbyes,
the brief-cased departure,
a long day stretching before her,
she flees to the shops,
vicarious companionship of crowded aisles,
spurious intimacy of sales girls.
She goes from counter to counter,
pricing, fingering. Boxes are delivered,
the business occupies an empty afternoon.
Next day she will take them back.

# A VILLANELLE FOR MONTAIGNE

How pleasant to go with Montaigne,
"The journey's the thing," he said,
not speeding through space in a plane

not even a car or a train
but a leisurely stage-coach instead.
How pleasant to go with Montaigne,

through the poplar-lined roads of Lorraine
by fields where poppies grow red,
not speeding through space in a plane.

To hear the welcome refrain
of bells from the village ahead.
How pleasant to go with Montaigne.

To start on our journey again,
refreshed and well wined and well fed,
not speeding through space in a plane.

A companion wise and urbane,
a Seigneur well-born and well-bred.
How pleasant to go with Montaigne
not speeding through space in a plane.

# VOYAGEUR

They saw the early morning of America,
the interminable forests
untouched by plundering hands.
Rivers for roadways,
their strength of arm
to lift and dip the paddles
shining in the sun,
they steered their frail craft
through turbulent white waters.
Their plaintive songs broke
the silence of the wilderness,
the flame of their camp-fires
lit the immensity of its dark.

# CHRISTMAS AT THE COUNTY HOME

They file by the jolly Santa Claus
in wheel chairs
or hobbling painfully on crutches.
The halls are decked with tinsel,
Merry Christmas glows in scarlet
on drab walls.
This spurious gayety brings no smile
to vacant faces or joy to hearts
remembering Christmases at home,
laughter of children
and the warmth of love.
But one sits in her room apart
and tries to keep alive
the Christmas spirit.
She lights a candle
and sings a carol
in a quavering voice.

# SPRING LAUGHTER

## SPRING LAUGHTER

The brook in spring, tumultuous, swift,
floods the bank on either side
sweeping the flotsam winter left
with its onrushing tide.

A child's laugh is a brook in May,
bubbling from a secret source,
bearing wintry thoughts away
on its cascading course.

# RIVER OF TIME

Once this river flowed smoothly,
one generation merging into another
with scarcely a ripple
to trouble the surface.
Now the current quickens,
swirls in treacherous eddies
around submerged rocks.
They who ride that torrent,
hearing the thunder of the waterfall
need skills unknown to those
who steered a well-charted course
on the tranquil waters
of time's slow-moving stream.

## SILENCE

Silence is not only lack of sound,
it is a balm for ears assaulted
by too frequent stridency.
Only in the silence after storm
could Elijah hear the still small voice
that brought fresh courage
to his flagging zeal.
So we, assailed by storm of words
and winds of controversy,
need stillness and a listening heart
for grace and for renewal.

# A PRICE TO PAY

High-rise apartments,
stark against the sky,
gas-pumps and bill-boards
catch the passing eye,
huge trucks thunder past,
like herds of mastodon,
belching clouds of smoke
that hide the sun.

In ages past man's works
enhanced the natural scene,
a Grecian temple on the rocks
above the sea, the ivied tower,
horses with a laden cart
plodding along a country road,
all these seemed to be part
of nature's plan.
Is ugliness the price
progress demands of man?

## THE HEALERS

The bulldozers have gone,
the new highway pours
its river of concrete
across the land.
Now on the gashed hillside
grass is spreading
covering with compassionate green
the scars of man's depredation.

Snow falls, flake on flake,
masking all ugliness,
the sordid alley, rusting car
shine in the morning sun,
swathed in white purity.

The wounds of earth are healed
by grass and snow.

# LITTERED

My mind is like a littered beach
that careless picnickers have left,
here an empty paper cup
once filled with high purpose,
here a half-eaten sandwich
of undigested facts,
a rotting banana of outworn prejudices.
Would that a wave might sweep it all away,
leaving it clean
like a beach at high tide.

# MIDDLE-AGE

This is a day to climb the hill,
see wind-swept clouds go scudding by,
leaves falling in cascades of flame,
woods in autumn panoply.

This is the day to climb the hill,
drunk with heady wine-sharp air.
But I will sit and drink my tea,
sunk in my favorite easy chair.

# THE GIFT OF SIGHT

I passed a blind man with his cane
and pausing, tried to realize
what life would be without my eyes,
then thankfully went on my way
savoring with keen delight
all that passed before my sight
that seemed not worth a glance before —
sunlight haloing the hair
of babies out to take the air,
and, oblivious to all,
two lovers lingering for a kiss
sequestered in their private bliss.

I studied faces as they passed
to guess what their expressions meant,
of happiness or discontent,
then paused before a shop to see
treasures of the world displayed,
silver, porcelain, ivory, jade,
and looking up saw on a roof
flowering trees shine in the sun
like the Hanging Gardens of Babylon.

I passed a blind man with his cane
and thought, how strange it was that he
had opened my dull eyes to see.

# LOST WONDER

The hillside with its crusted snow
shone smooth and glistening in the sun,
"Just like the hill of glass", I said,
"the princess dwelt upon".
With an uncomprehending stare
the child looked up at me,
"I don't read fairy tales" she scoffed,
"I always watch T.V."

Defrauded child! My mind turned back
to the absorbing hours spent
with Anderson and Brothers Grimm,
whose tales of wonder lent
enchantment to my youthful world.
Happy the children who have stood
tiptoe with eagerness to see
fairies in the wood.

## MOTEL TALK — ON THE ROAD

What kind of a car do you drive?
How many miles did you make?
Where did you come from,
how long did it take?
Did you try the new thruway,
did you find it good?
Where did you stop for lunch,
how was the food?
None spoke of seeing
the little sun-lit pond
where water-lilies
floated, and beyond
a solitary heron
standing in the sedge,
or the hawk sailing high
above the distant ridge.
None spoke of smelling balsam
as they traveled north,
or mentioned the varied flowers
on the abundant earth.

## PSALM FOR THE SUN

The rains are over,
the great sun climbs the sky.
Centuries fall away
and I am a sun worshipper.
This is no ball of burning gas
but a god, dazzling in splendor,
mighty in power,
without him all on earth would perish,
at his touch mountains leap unto light,
sap rises in the tree,
the seed quickens to life.
At his coming birds wake and sing
and small insects dance in his beams.
He takes his way across the heavens
and the gates of the west
flame at his passing.
Great is he and worthy
to be worshipped.

# HOMESICK

There is a malady
no medicine can cure,
no surgery can cut the ache
out of the homesick heart.
Unbidden, in an alien land,
will flash a scene of home
and the spirit is engulfed
in waves of pain.
For some the scene
will be a city square,
for some a cabin
by a mountain lake.
And some will hear in dreams
the sound of surf
and some the blue jay's call
on an October day.
For every man holds in his heart
one corner of the earth,
familiar and dear,
that calls to him
wherever he may be.

## THE MOUNTAIN OF LIFE

The approach lies through flowering meadows
beside the singing stream.
The path is smooth, guides point the way.
Now the mountain looms ahead,
the summit lost in clouds.
The trail grows rougher,
often hard to find,
but there are glades in which to rest,
bird-song and the scent of pine.
Sometimes a rift in the clouds
shows glimpses of that far land
beyond the summit and the heart
is given new strength for climbing.
The way grows steeper near the top,
limbs fail, breath falters,
few are left of the companions of the trail.
Obstacles passed on the lower slopes
diminish at that great height.
The last assault is made alone,
the summit reached
and that new country glimpsed before
revealed and bathed in light.

# JUNE COMMENCEMENT

There is the scent of lilacs
and of fresh-cut grass,
a froth of white dresses,
the sound of laughter and of young voices
rises on air tense with expectancy.
How young, how vulnerable they seem
in the pride of this hour,
carrying diplomas like a sword
to meet the challenges ahead.
With tightened throats parents watch
remembering their youth
and the framed diploma
relegated to the attic.

## "BY HEART"

"Elocution", they called it
in those by-gone school days,
memorizing and reciting a poem.
What patience you had, Miss Bennet,
how it must have grated on your ears
to hear the words fall so haltingly
from our stumbling lips.
You taught us well, Miss Bennet,
years pass but the poems remain,
lofty summits rising above life's trivia,
or lilting music to fill an empty hour
or calm a time of stress.

# BALLAD OF THE TITANIC

The ship sailed out in all her pride
while pennants fluttered and whistles blew,
the fastest ship to take the tide,
"She'll break the record", said her crew.

The sea was smooth and the moon shone bright,
the passengers danced in the gay saloon
and a pair of lovers stood that night
hand in hand to watch the moon.

The woman shivered as she spoke
"It's grown much colder suddenly,
please go below and get my cloak
but hurry and come back to me."

He kissed and left her standing there,
the cabin was three decks below,
the moonlight shone upon her hair,
she shivered as she watched him go.

The captain knew there was ice ahead
but though he knew he paid no heed.
"Break the record" was what they said,
he told the crew to keep up speed.

She saw a sudden phantom loom
with pinnacles of glistening white,
a mammoth thing, a shape of doom
drifting through the silent night.

Too late, too late, to slow up then,
too late for passengers and crew.
the lovers never met again,
the gallant ship was cut in two.

Dark is the night and cold the wave
and sleep is long in a watery grave.

## ONLY HERE

Silence, once the common coin of life,
is now a golden nugget to be found
only by patient search.  The quiet lake,
where drip of paddles was the only sound,
now echoes to the din of motor boats.
Sno-mobiles, roaring through winter woods,
disturb the hush of softly falling snow.
Yet still on mountain summits silence broods
as through the aeons of primordial time.
Here in the tranquil majesty of space,
above the noise, the conflicts and confusions,
peace fills the heart with its abiding grace.

## ON THE ROAD

It was a long hill
and a winding road,
no room to pass the truck
that labored up the grade.
I cursed the truck and the delay
then looked about me as I crept along.
Bobolinks rose from a daisy field
in a cascade of song.
In the cleft of a rocky ledge
columbines found a precarious hold,
sunlight filtered through the leaves
and far off, fold on fold
hills were a haze of amethyst.
With lifted heart I blessed the truck
for all the loveliness
I might have missed.

# SPIRIT OF THE HOUSE

A house is more than wood and stone,
it holds the distillate of emotions
felt within its walls,
intangible in air.

I crossed the threshold
of a stranger's house
and sensed at once
that here was harmony.
Love with its immortal grace
had touched this mortal place.

In a palace in a foreign land
where an unhappy queen
had been imprisoned,
the sorrow still held captive
in that room was like a chilling wind.
I could not linger there
but hastened out
into the welcome sun.

A house is more than wood and stone.

## UNTAINTED

I marveled that water,
traveling underground,
domain of mole and worm,
passing through black earth,
decaying root,
could gush forth from this spring
so crystal clear.
So there are those who pass
through the world
assailed on every side
by lust and knavery
yet never lose their purity.

# LIGHT VERSE

# AL FRESCO

"Bringing their lunch to eat outside is
becoming popular with New Yorkers."
— *N. Y. Times*

How nice to eat your ham and rye on
the Library steps beside the lion,
or high on a girder, a tiny speck,
with no one breathing down your neck,
watching hungrily while you eat,
waiting to grab your empty seat.

They wait in no slow moving line
who sit in Bryant Park to dine.
Scornful of waiters or bill-of-fare
are those who eat in the open air.

## DILEMMA

There are two adages I ponder.
"Absence makes the heart grow fonder"
and "Out of sight is out of mind"
are contradictory I find.
Suppose I were to travel far
to Timbuctoo or Zanzibar
thinking while I was away
you'd grow more ardent every day;
only to find I'd not been missed
and you'd forgotten I exist,
whereas, if I'd not left your side,
with luck, by now I'd be your bride.

# MODERN WITCHING

The love-sick maid of long ago
sought out a witch at dead of night
and by the bubbling cauldrons glow
begged for help in her sad plight.

She bought love philters for her need,
learned incantations and a spell
which the old hag had guaranteed
would make her irresistible.

But love-lorn maidens of today
make no appointment with a witch,
to learn their spells the girls can stay
at home and merely turn a switch.

From honied voices on the air
they learn all that they need to know
of dazzling teeth and gleaming hair
and hints on how to snare a beau.

## KITCHEN ALCHEMY

I should wear a long black robe
and a tall and pointed hat,
like the alchemists of old
in their eager search for gold,
muttering weird incantations
for their secret transmutations
of this substance into that.

For I feel akin to them
when ingredients I take
to my complete surprise
become a cake!

# TRIOLET FOR AN UNMECHANICAL HOUSEWIFE

The thing won't work, what shall I do?
Directions don't seem very clear
they haven't given me a clue.
The thing won't work, what shall I do,
push a button or turn a screw?
I wish the service man was here.
The thing won't work, what shall I do?
Directions don't seem very clear.

# THE MODERN LOVER TO HIS LOVE

Come live with me and be my love
and I will do my best to prove
that two can live as cheap as one
and have considerably more fun.

Our life will be no bed of roses,
I'll work until the office closes
and you will cook and wash and iron
and make the bed for us to lie on.

But Saturdays we'll have a whirl,
dressed in your rope of Woolworth pearl,
with high-heeled shoes and your best gown
I'll take you out to do the town.

The movie stars will dance and sing
for our delight and I will bring
a chocolate bar so we can sit
holding hands and eating it.

Next morning we can lie abed
till all the Sunday news is read.
If these delights your doubts remove
then live with me and be my love.

# IMPERFECT PARADISE

Wake, for the coffee bubbles in the pot,
the egg is waiting and the toast is hot,
this is no day for lingering in bed
we must be up and dig our garden plot.

Sometimes I think that never flower grows
that blooms as long or smells as sweet as those
so glowingly portrayed in catalogues.
Why do ours never look the same? Who knows?

Eager to learn, I zealously frequent
the garden club and hear great argument
concerning pesticides but evermore
come out as ignorant as in I went.

Ah, my beloved, if our garden seed
could grow and bloom with never any weed,
with never any blight or worm or slug
our garden would be Paradise indeed.

# NOVEMBER RESPITE

No need to spray to kill some pest
that winter's cold will slaughter,
the garden has been put to rest
no need to weed or water.

Now we can have a holiday
from shovel, hoe and rake,
the lawn-mower is put away
my back has ceased to ache.

A respite brief, but oh how sweet,
from any kind of chores
before we're battling snow and sleet
and struggling with storm doors.

# SEED CATALOGUES

No song of early robin,
no peeper in the bog
is such a harbinger of spring
as the first seed catalogue.

The frost may bite, the snow may fall,
the winter winds may freeze,
but here is all of summer's wealth
to choose from as we please.

Tomatoes, red and succulent,
crisp lettuce firm and green,
cabbage, beet and cucumber,
asparagus and bean.

Flowers, gay and colorful
in all their varied hues,
a knotty problem faces us
deciding which to choose.

And so, although we know full well
our garden plot is small,
we cut the knot with reckless pen
by ordering them all.